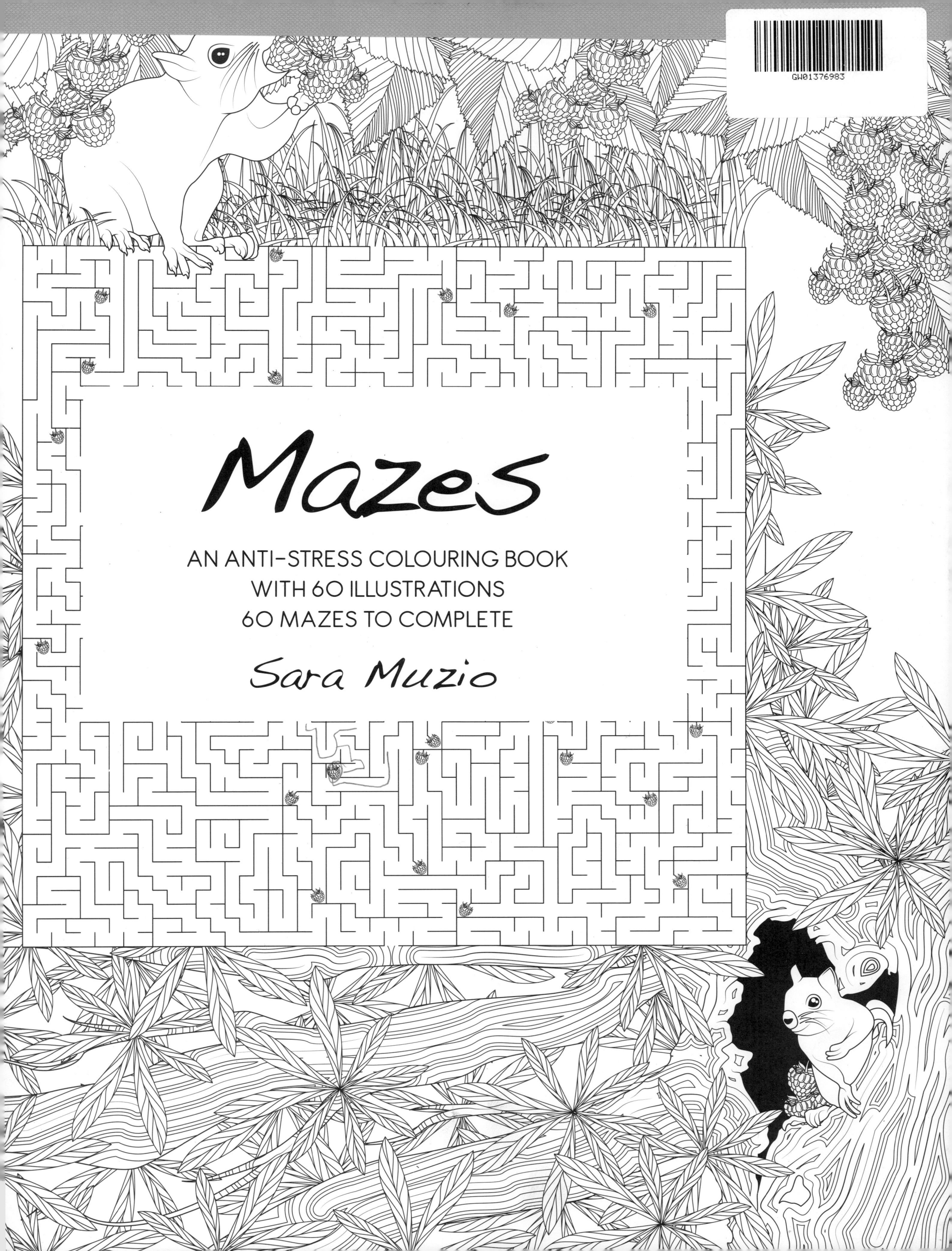

Mazes

AN ANTI-STRESS COLOURING BOOK
WITH 60 ILLUSTRATIONS
60 MAZES TO COMPLETE

Sara Muzio

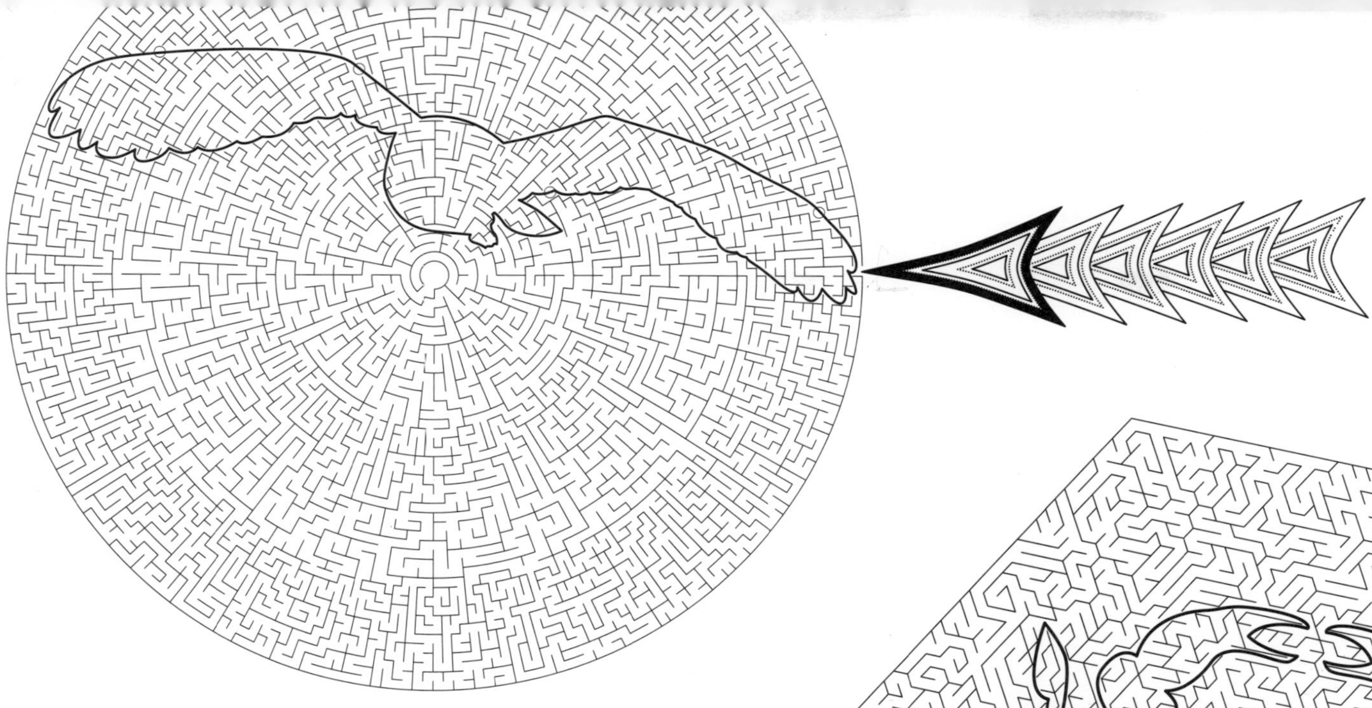

Test yourself on the mazes of
each table: trace the path starting
from the point indicated by the
arrow and return to the starting
point, also with the assistance
of the dots you meet along the
way. At the end, you will find
out the animal's shape hiding
in the maze.

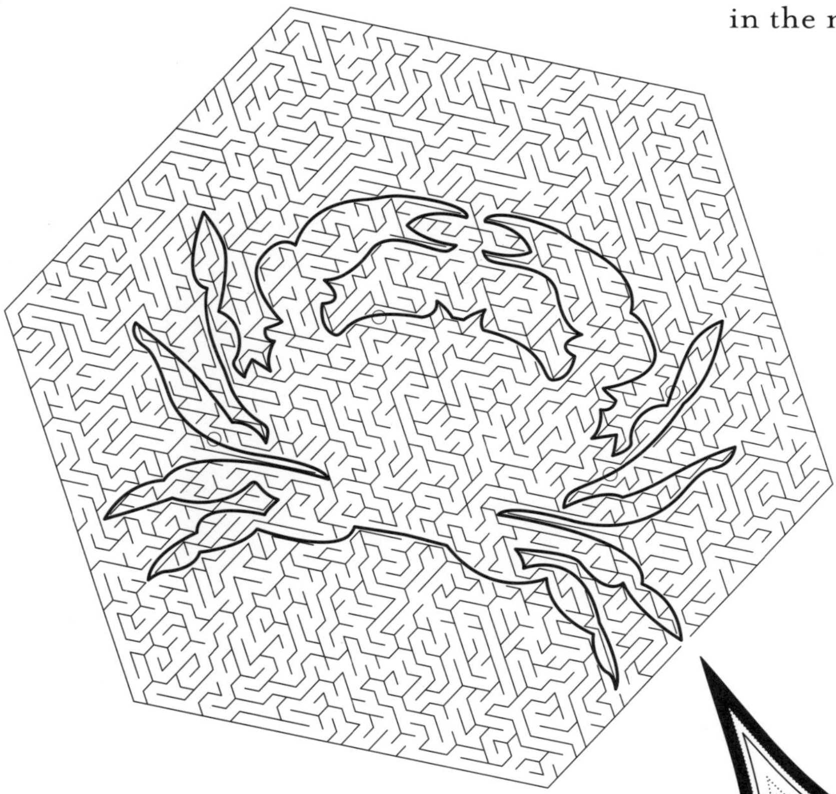

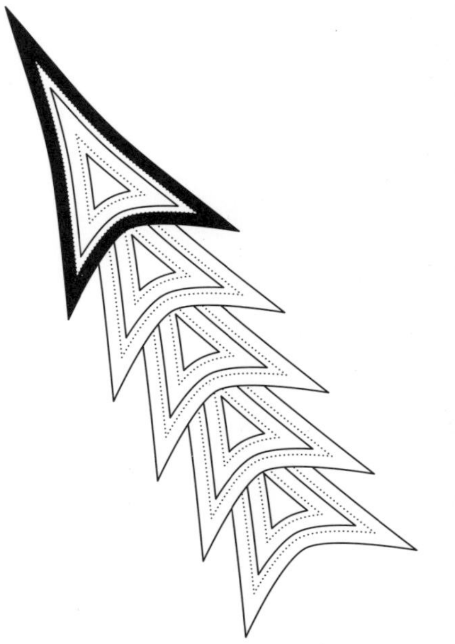

SARA MUZIO

Sara Muzio has over ten years of
experience working in graphic design
and illustration. In 2002, after earning
a degree in Medical Illustration, she
began working for small graphic design
studios and in 2004 she became the scientific illustrator
for Lumen Edizioni, where she completed a postgraduate course on
publishing and advertising graphics. From 2005 to 2011, Sara worked as a freelance
graphic designer for private clients as well as public entities and publishing houses. From
2011 to 2013, she was the graphic and packaging designer for Sambonet Paderno Industrie
S.p.A. She currently works as an illustrator and freelance graphic designer. In addition to
the illustrations found in this book, she created those for "Flower Fantasy - An Anti-stress
Colouring Book with 60 Illustrations", "Hidden in the Jungle - An Anti-stress Colouring
Book with 60 Illustrations", "The Extraordinary Journey of a Little Goldfish - Anti-stress
Colouring Book", "Zen Gardens - An Anti-stress Colouring Book with 60 Illustrations",
"A Fanstastic Journey among the Constellations - An Anti-stress Colouring Book with
60 Illustrations", "Metamorphosis - Anti-stress Colouring Book", "Day and Night,
Journey into the Secrets of Nature - Anti-stress Colouring Book", "The Perfect Cat"
and "A Fantastic Journey along Swallow Migratory Routes - Anti-stress Colouring Book"
for White Star Publishers.

GRAPHIC LAYOUT
Valentina Giammarinaro

COVER GRAPHIC DESIGN
Michela Barbonaglia

WS White Star Publishers® is a registered trademark property of White Star s.r.l.

© 2017 White Star s.r.l.
Piazzale Luigi Cadorna, 6 - 20123 Milan, Italy
www.whitestar.it

ISBN 978-88-544-1131-9
1 2 3 4 5 6   21 20 19 18 17

Printed in China

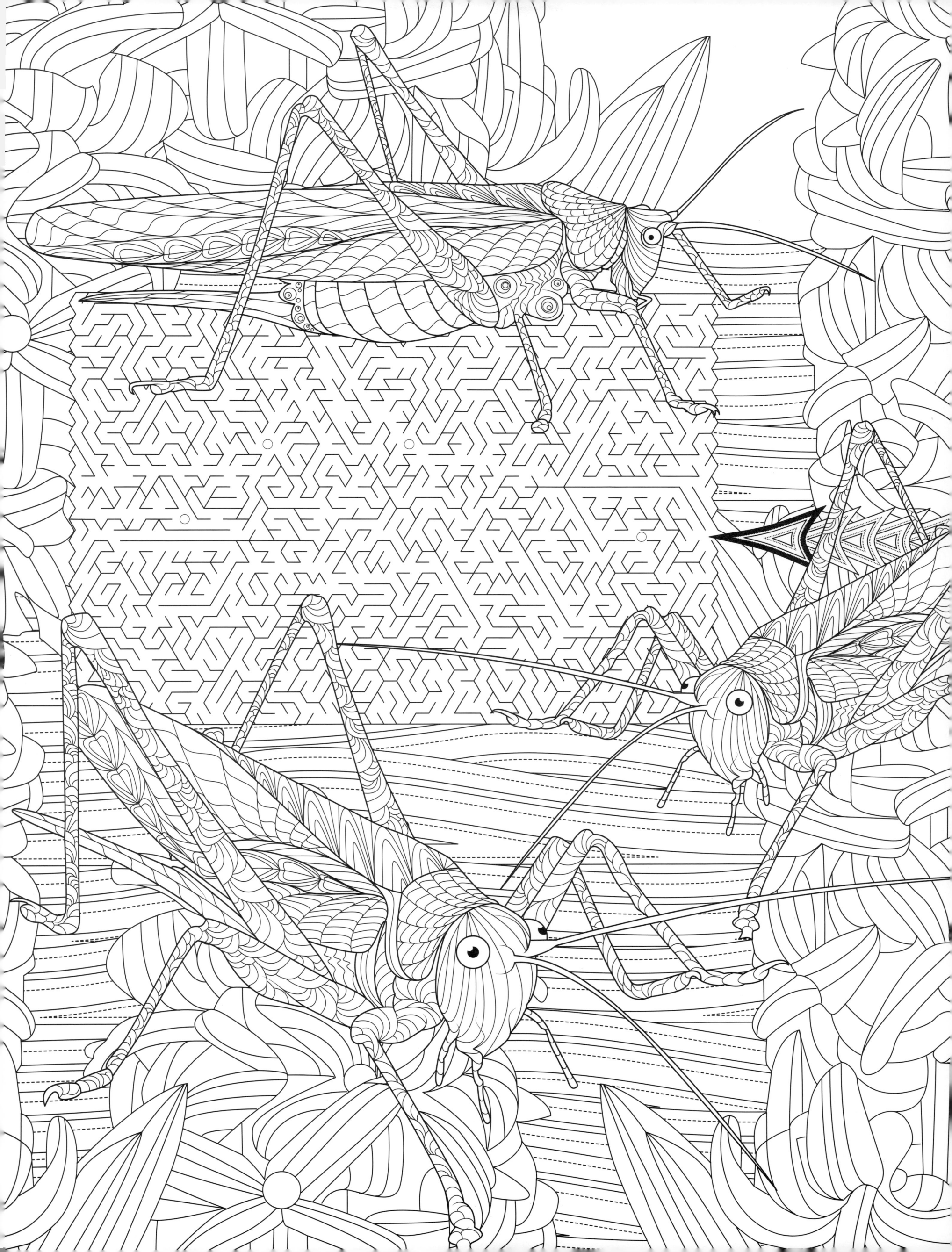

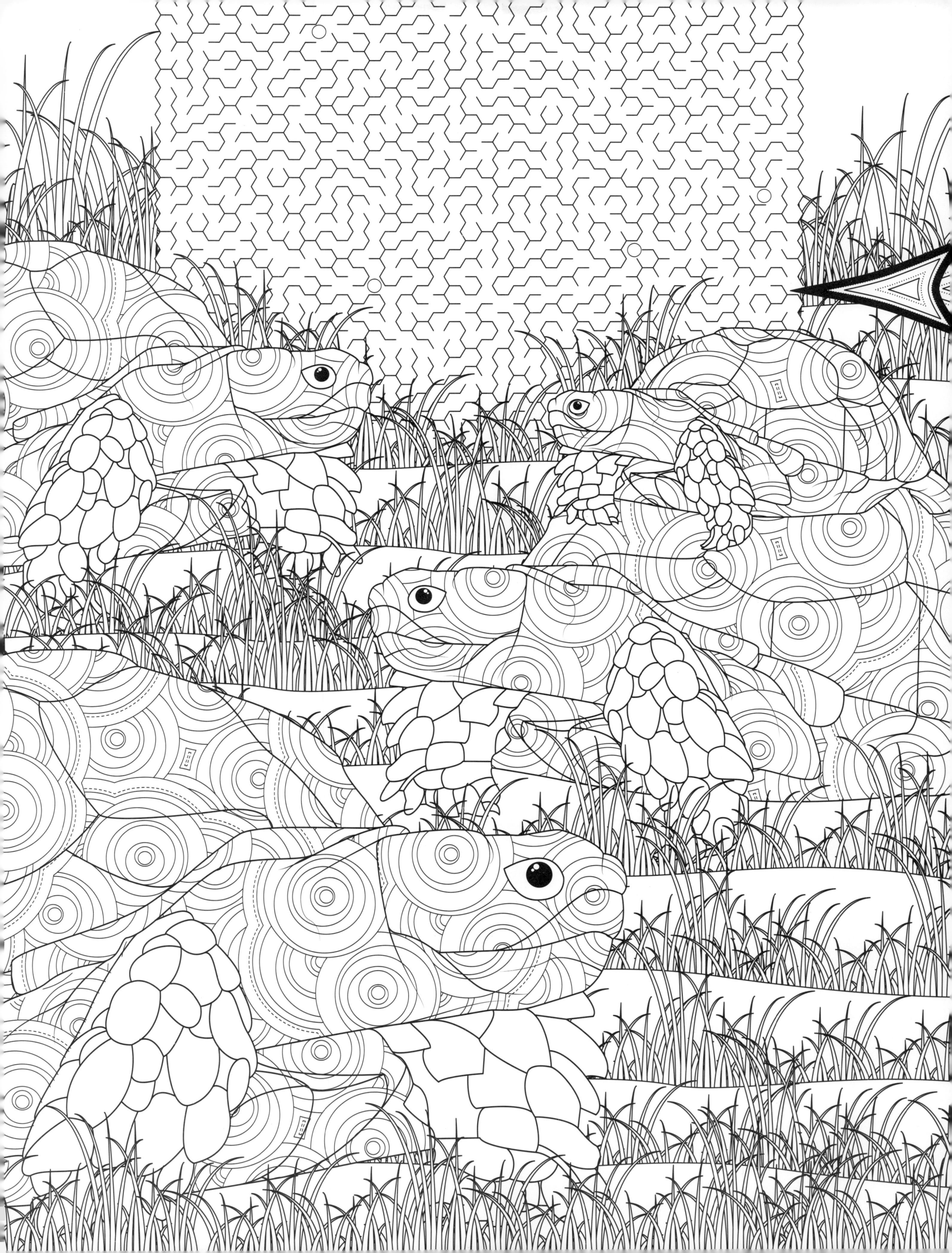

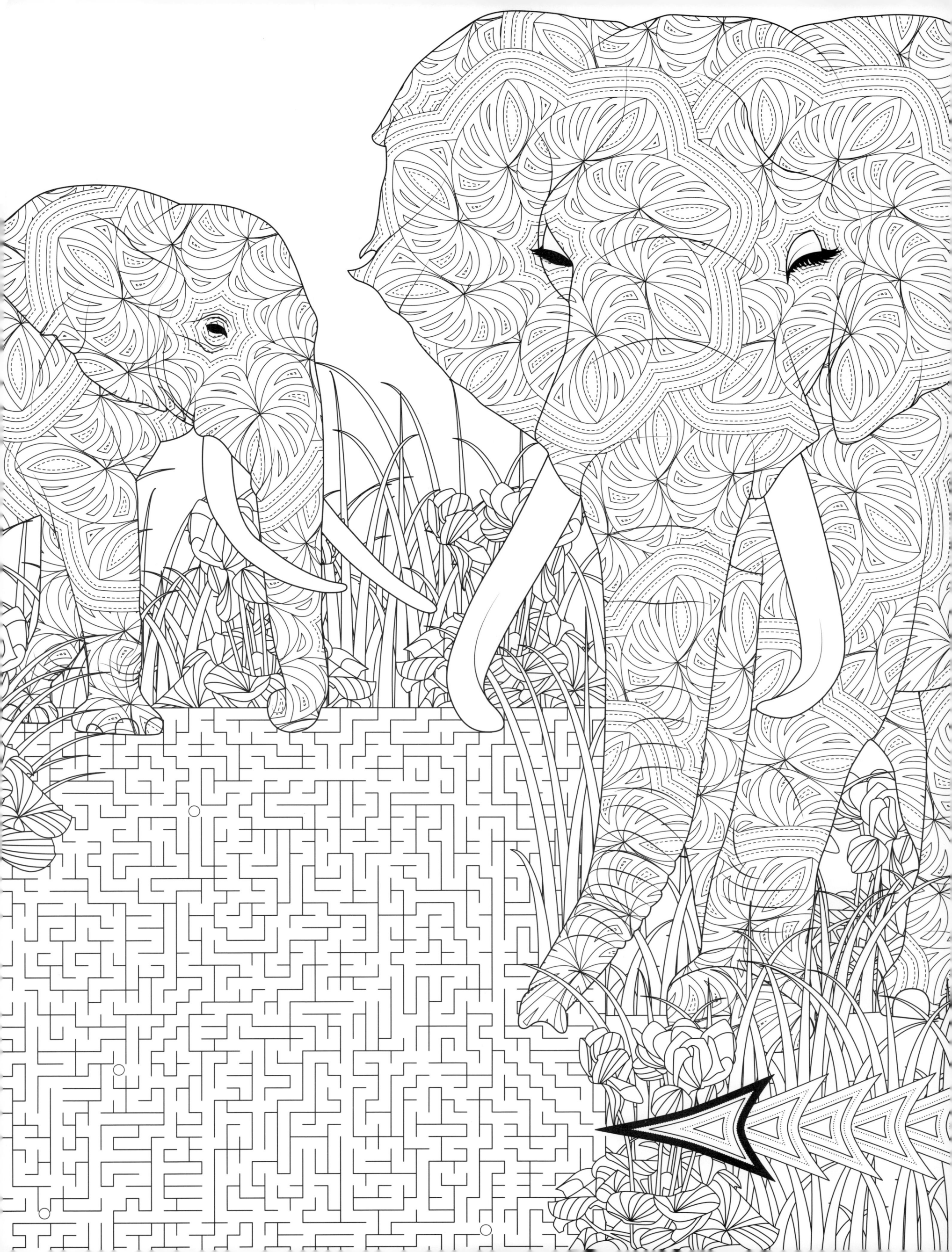

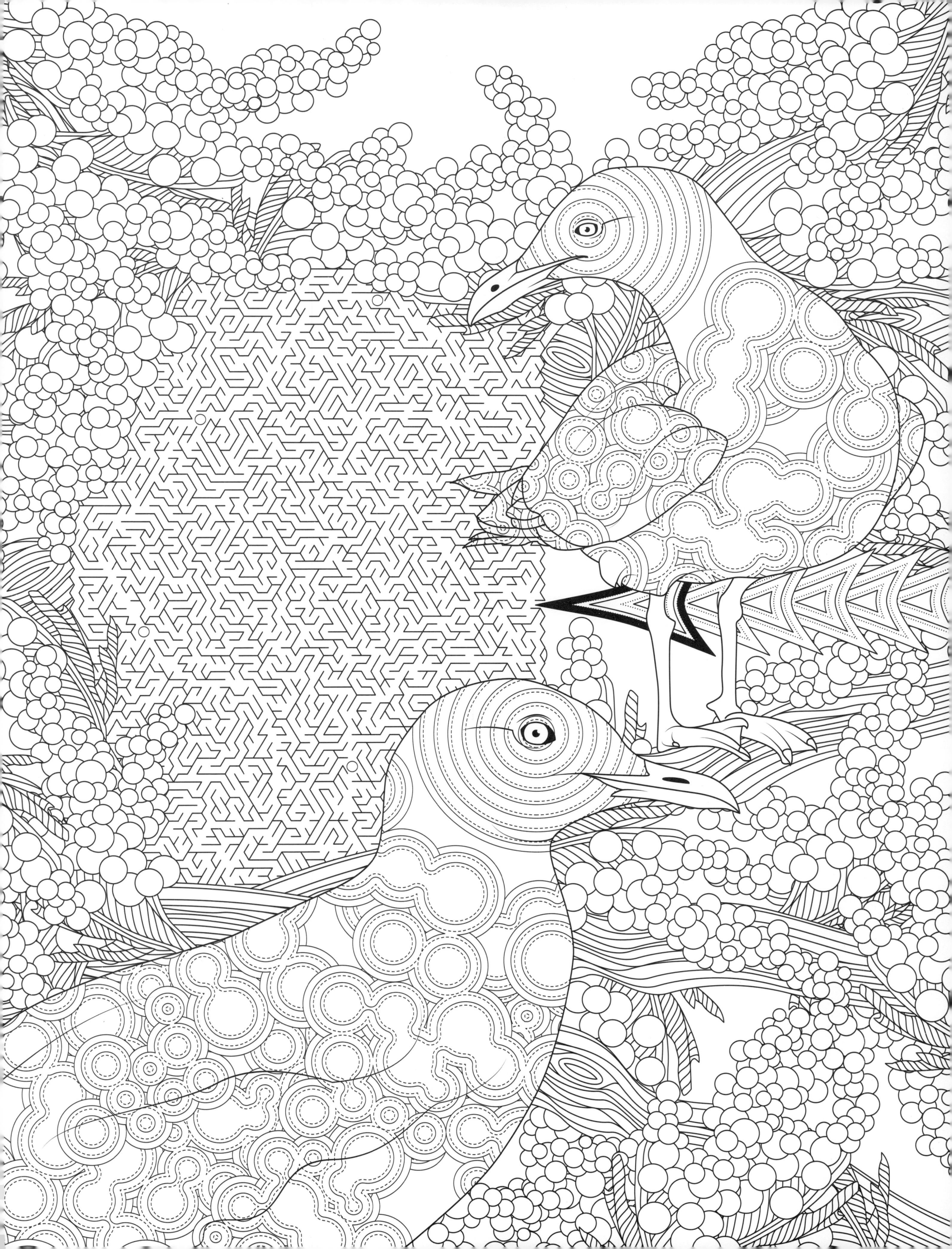

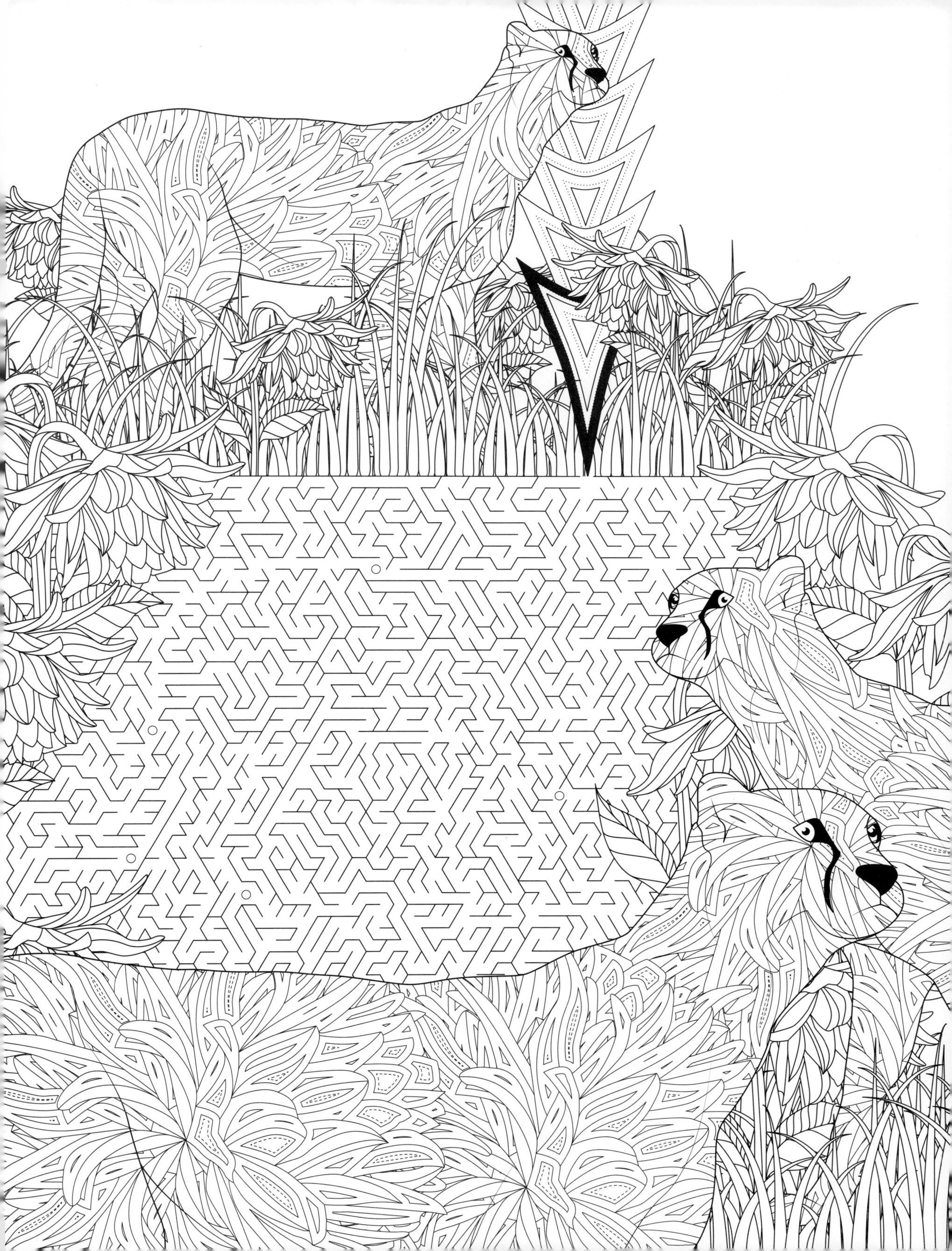

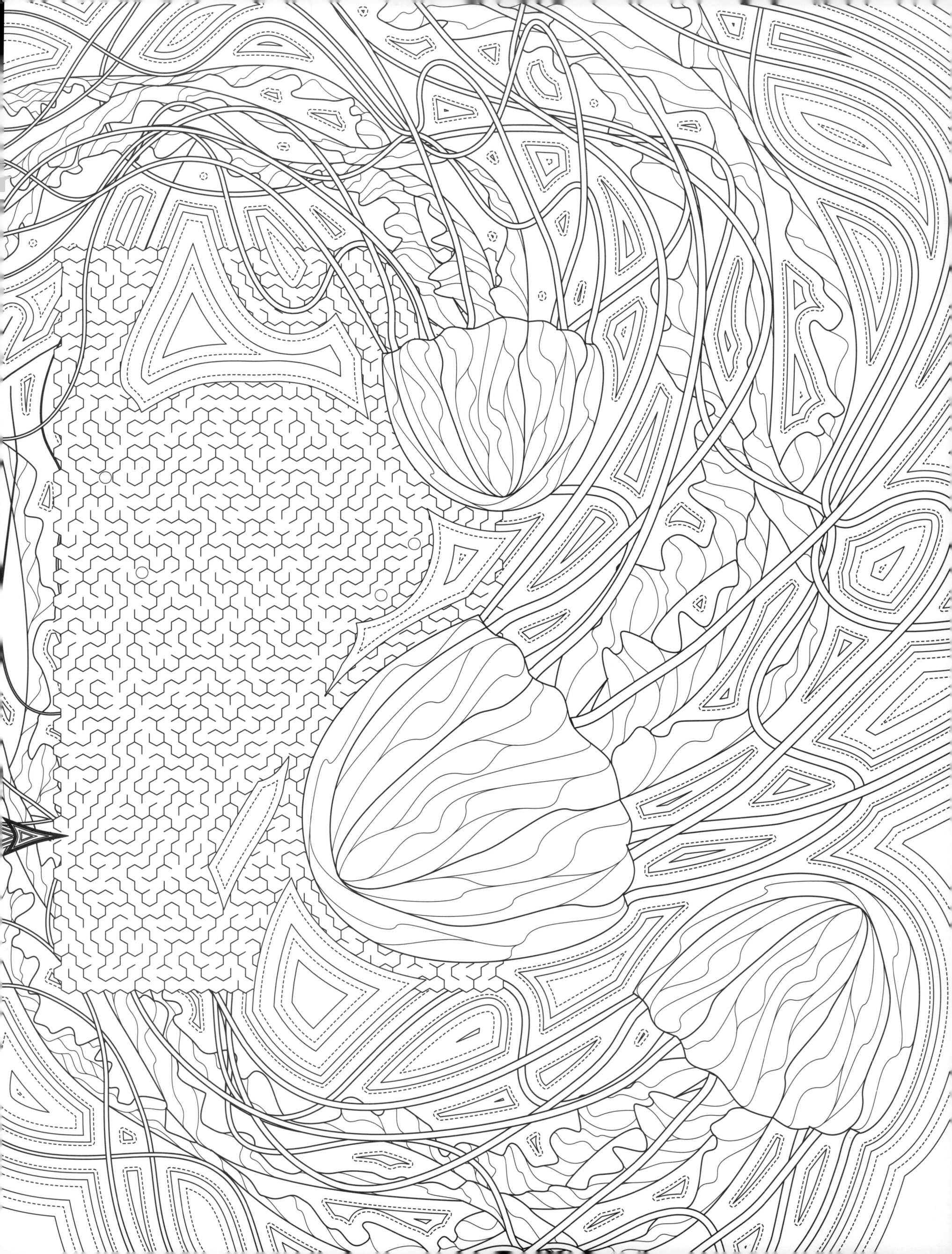

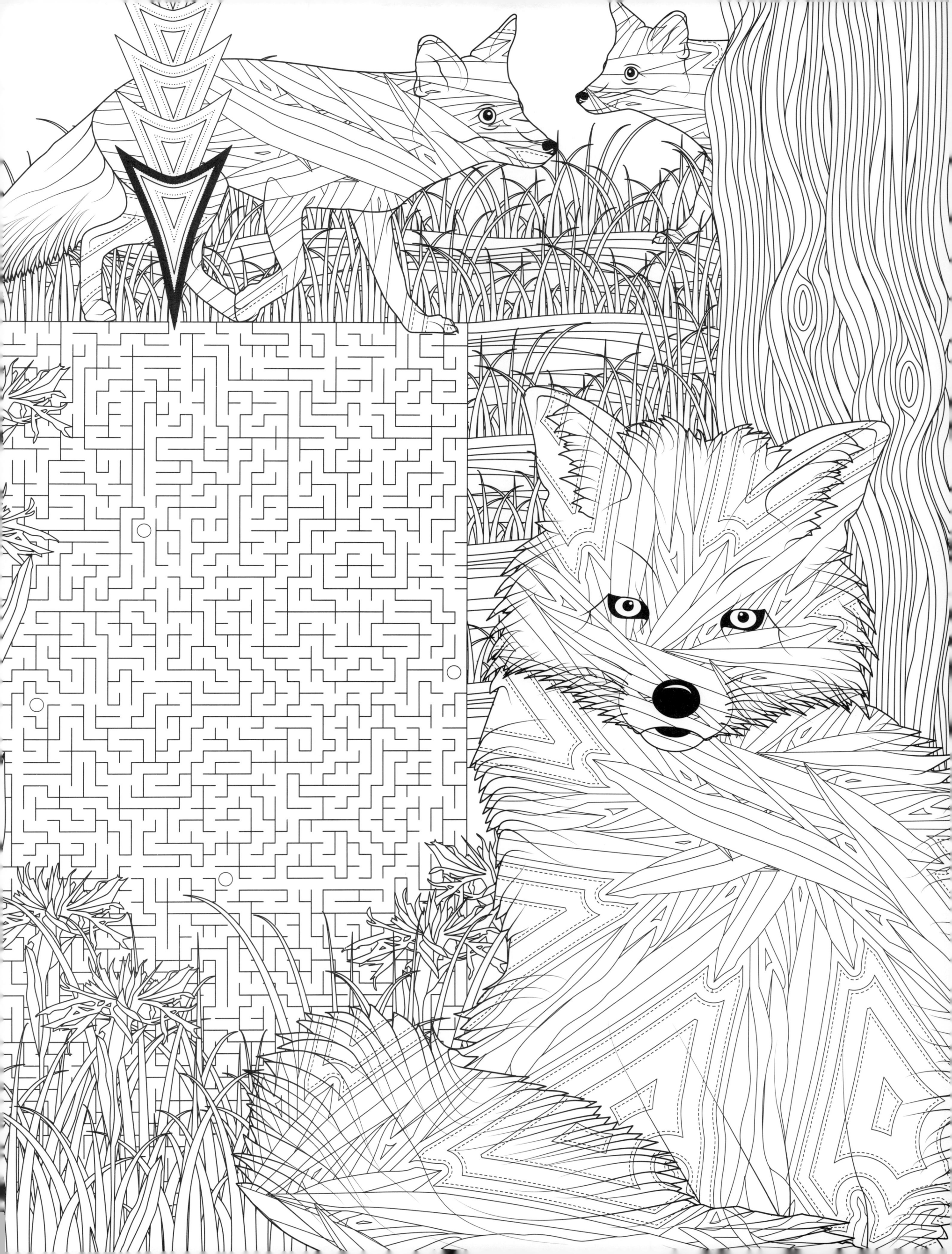

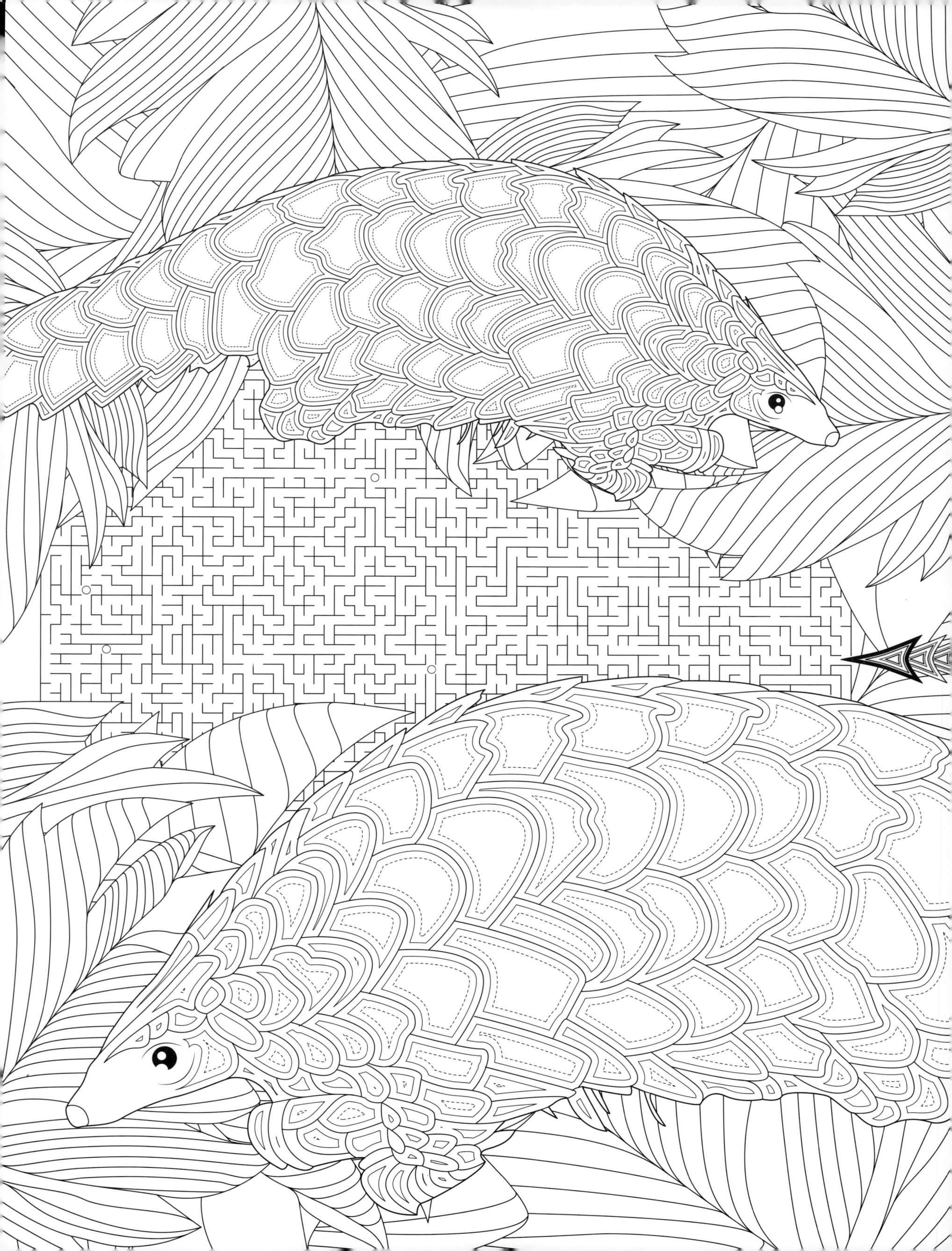

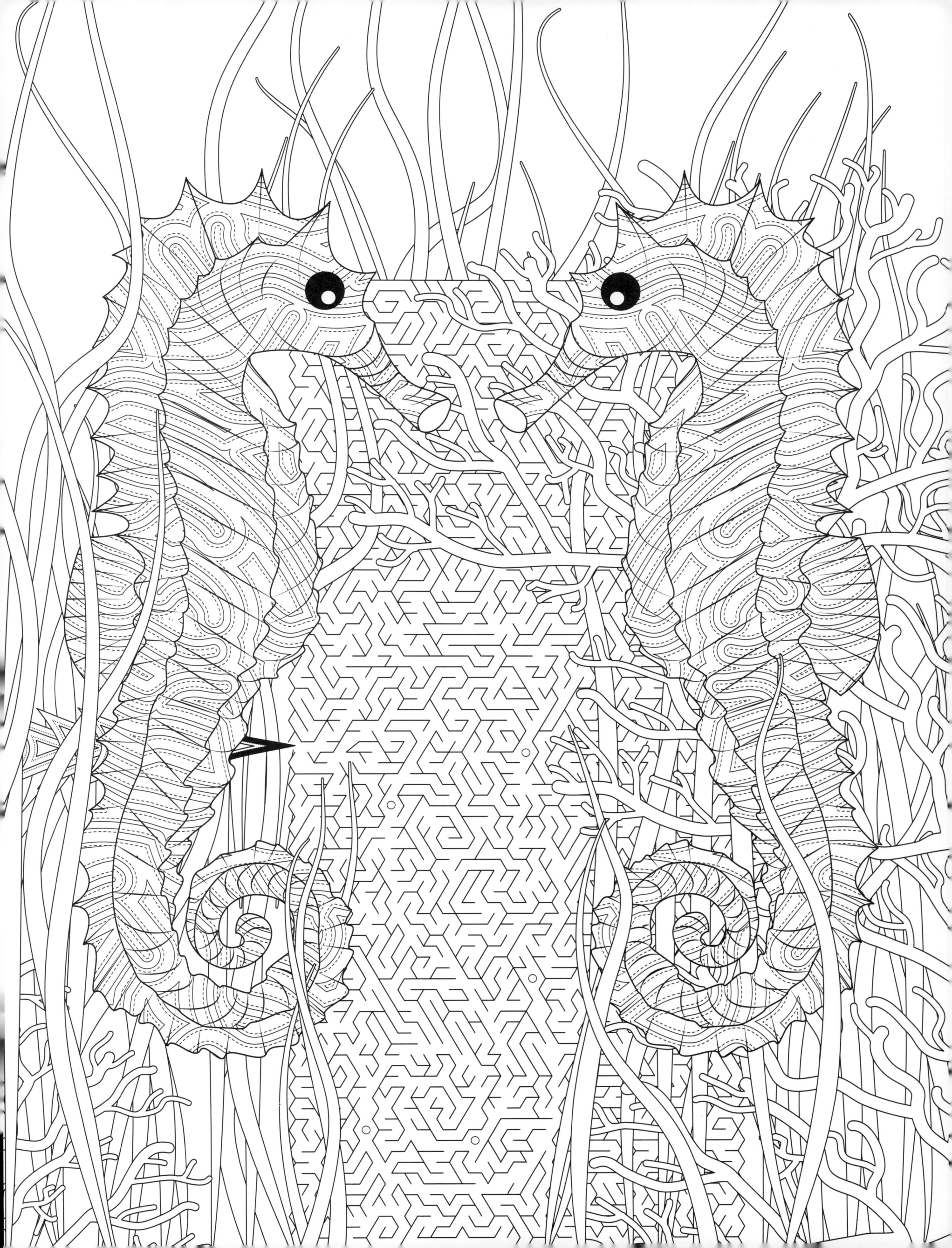

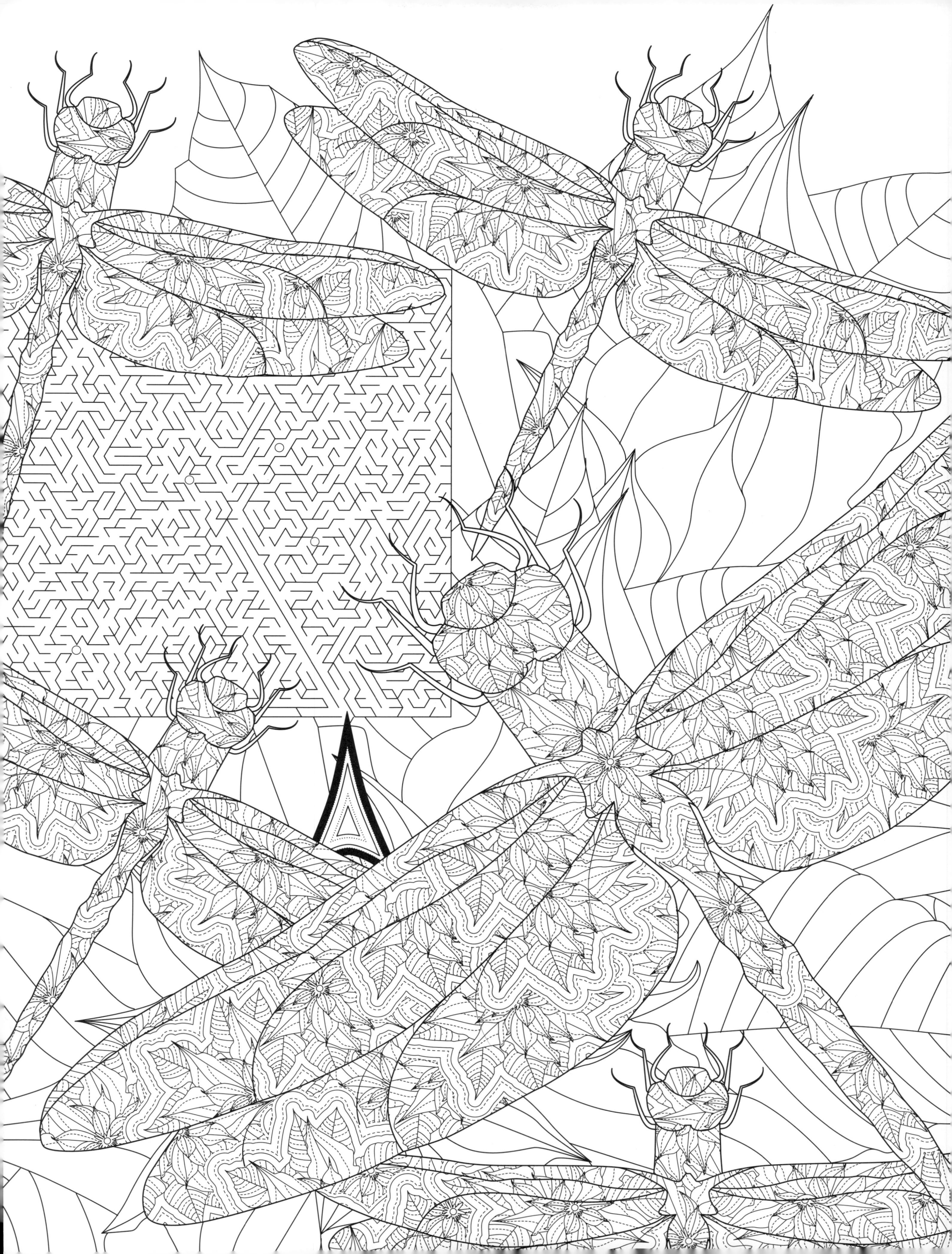

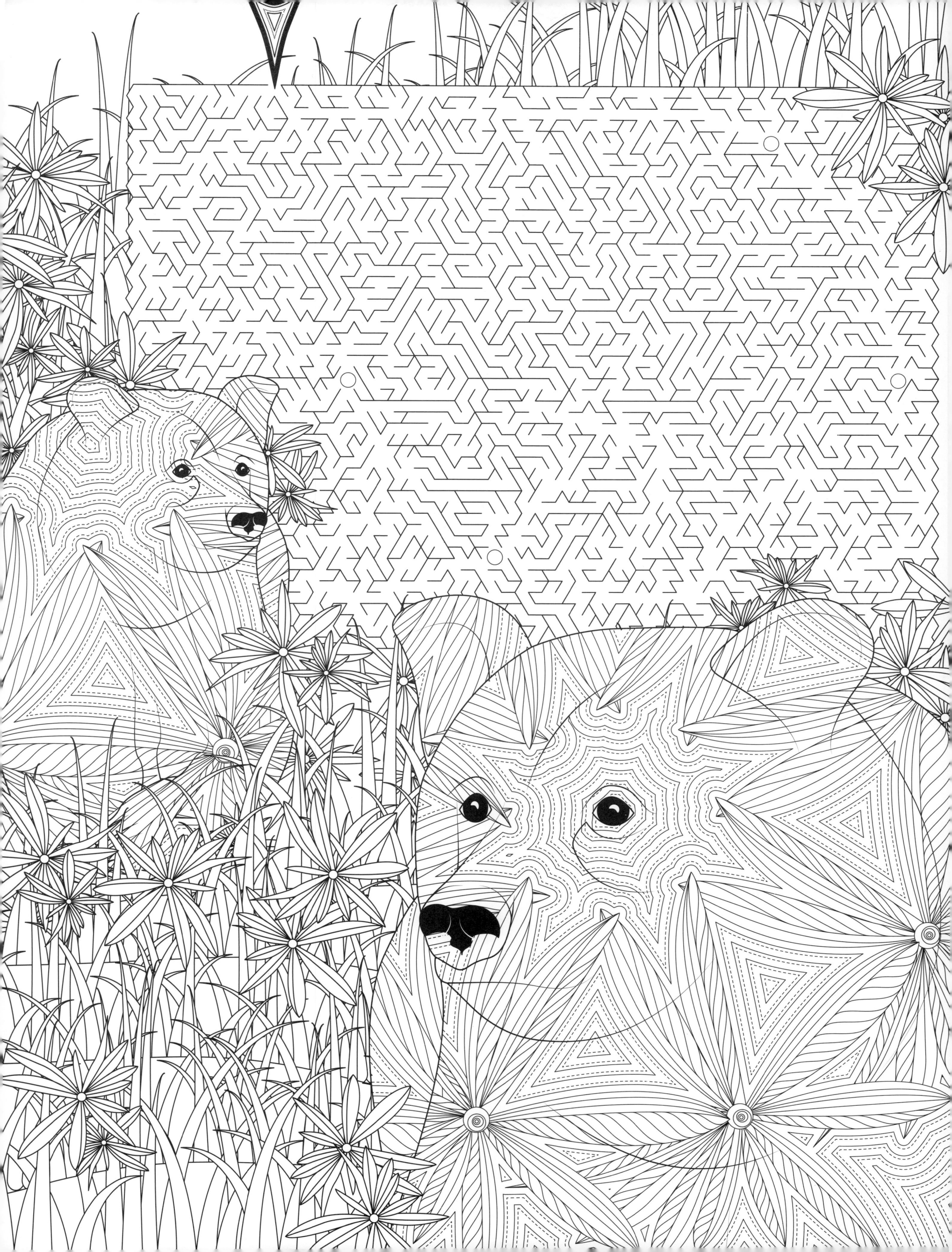

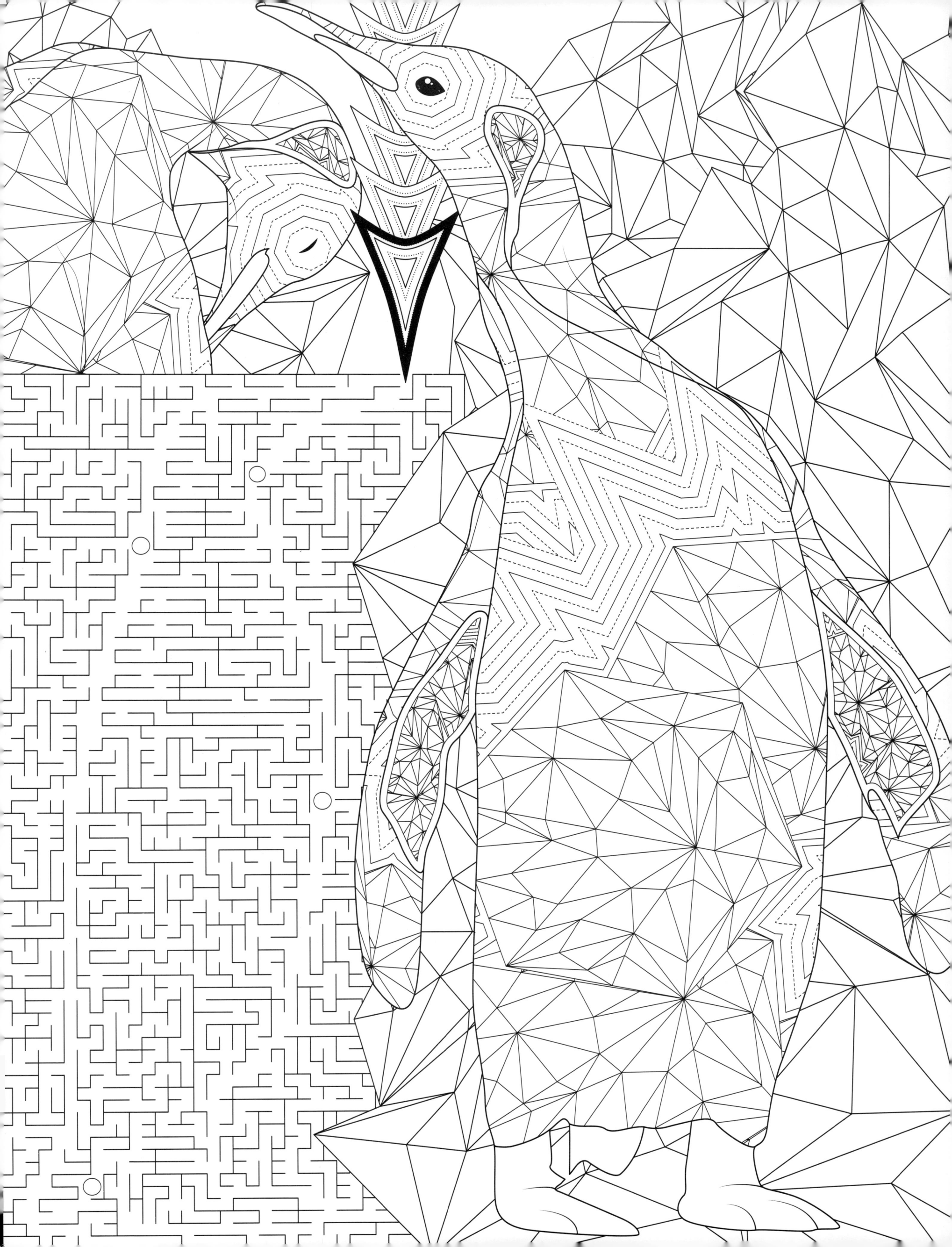

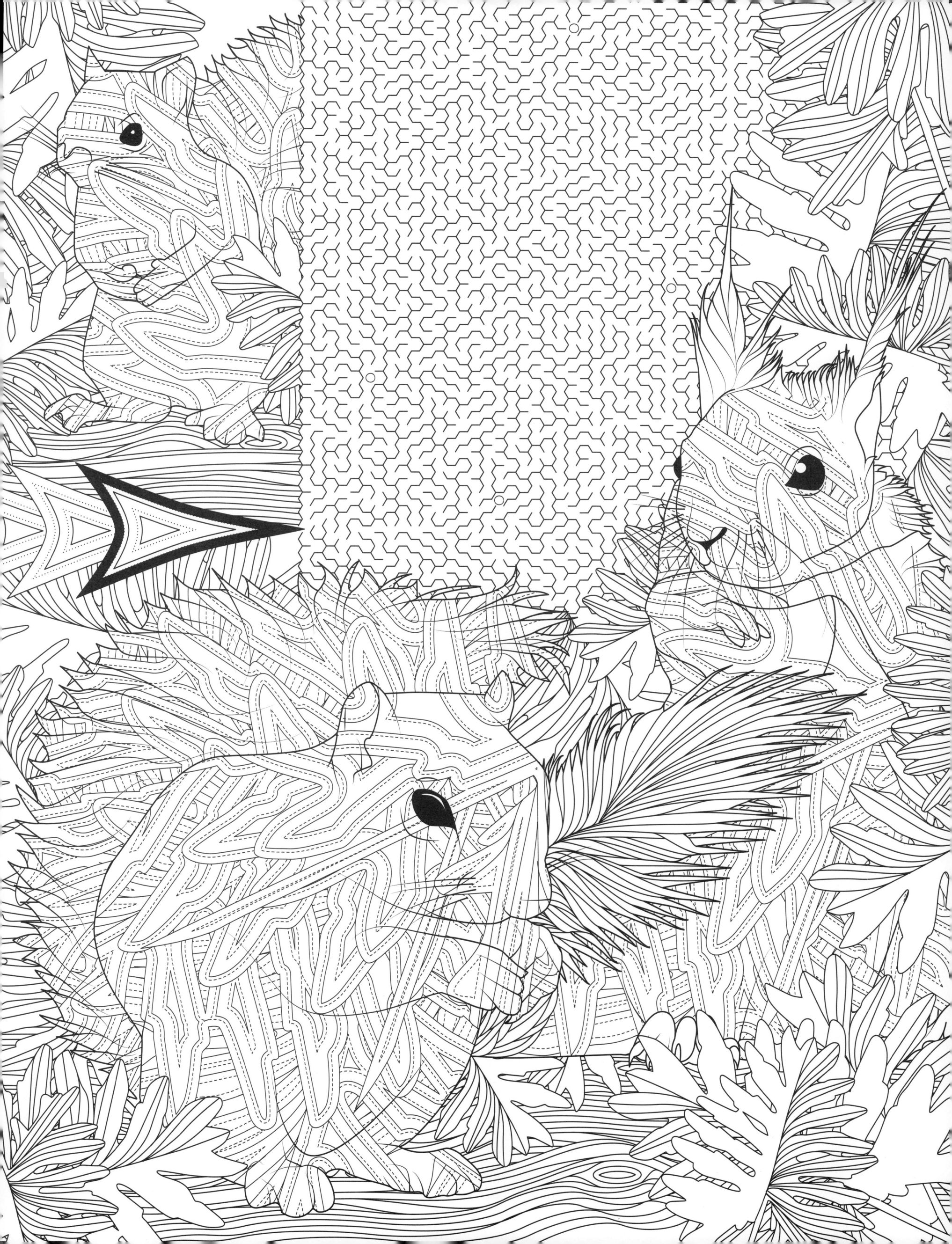

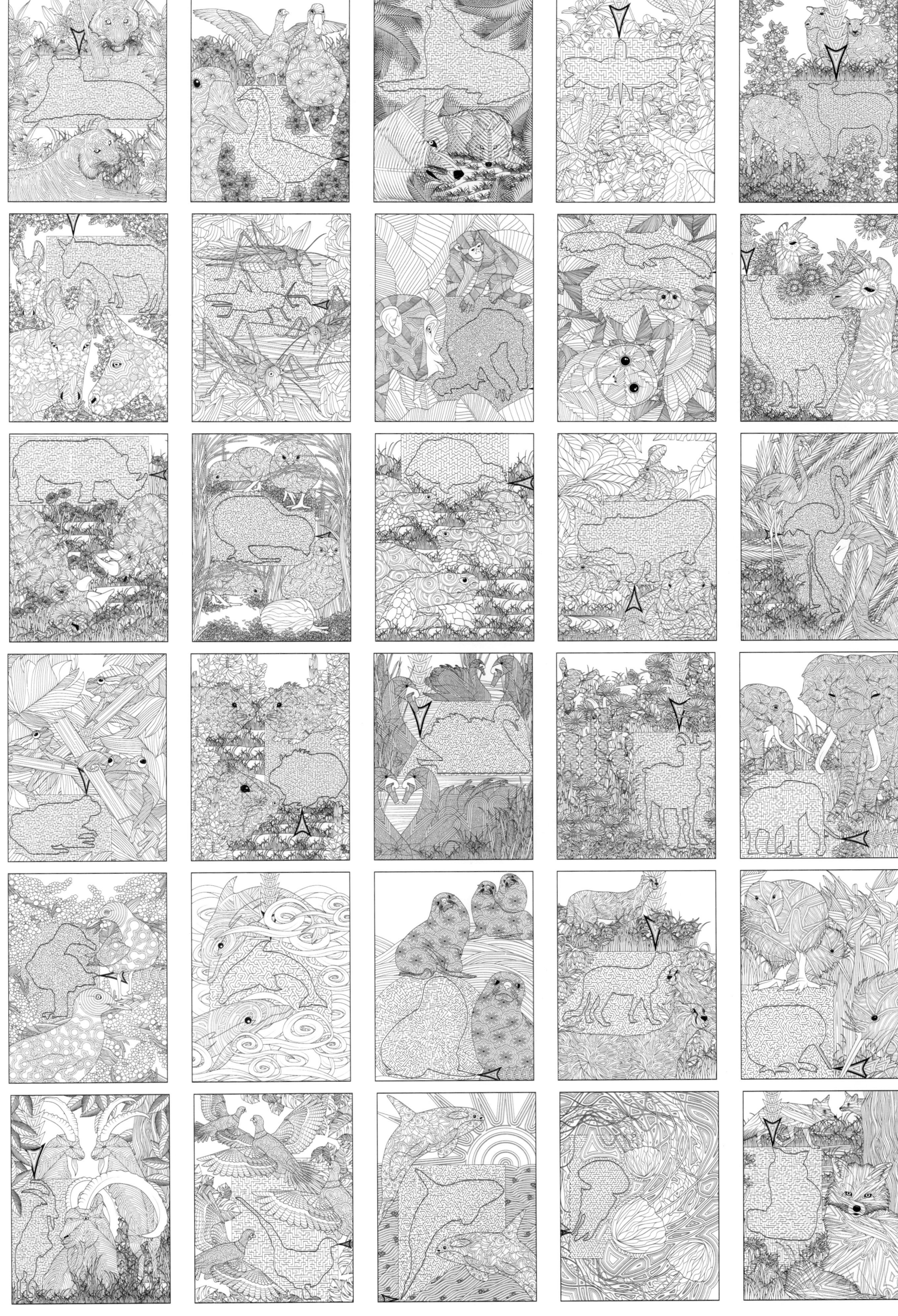

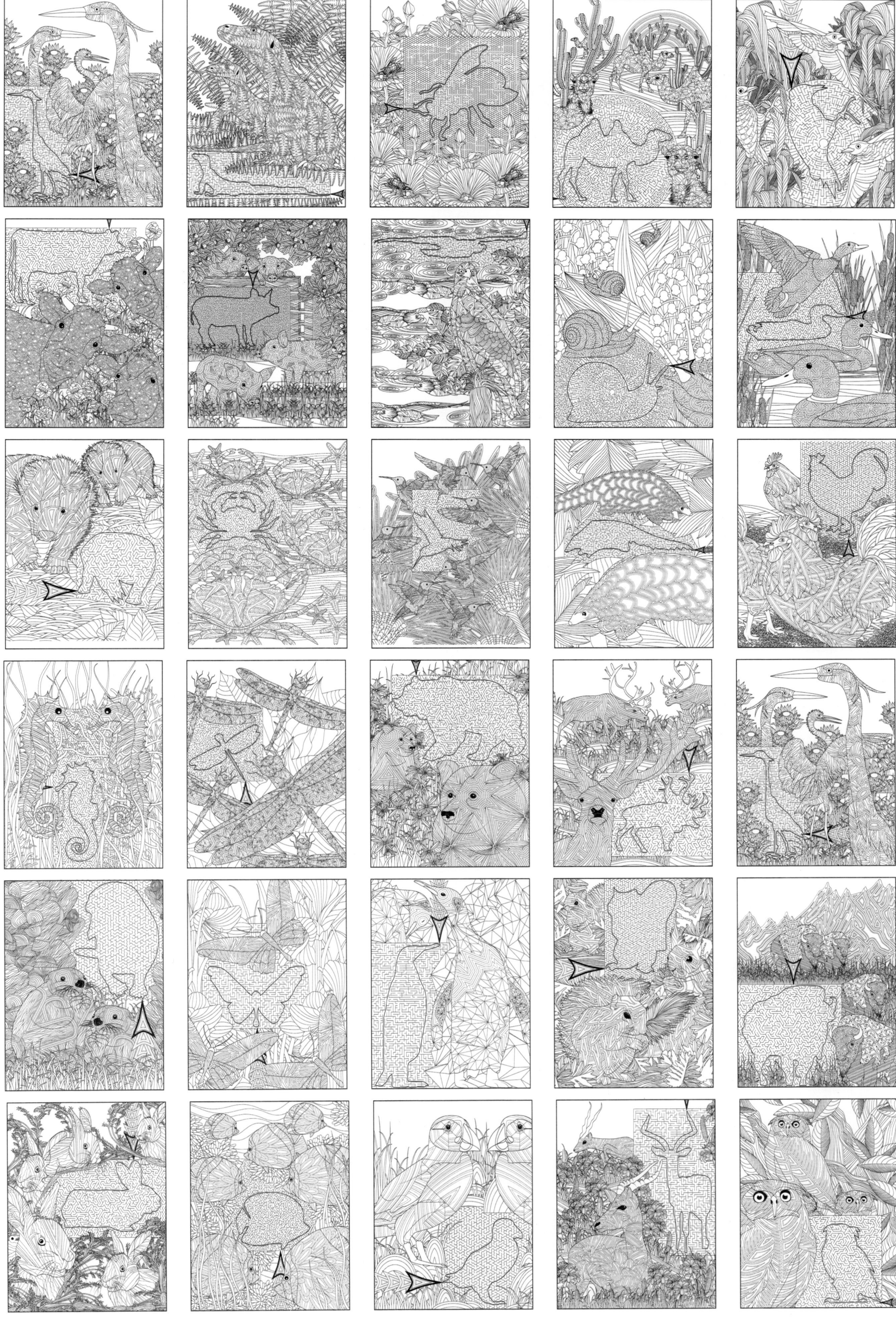